WHY CAN'T I FIGURE THIS MARKETING Thing Out?

Tonya Franklin
AUTHOR

Publisher:
Imani Blue Books & Press
Jackson, Mississippi

Imanibluebooks.com
imanibluebooks@gmail.com

Table of Contents

Lack of Understanding

Do you know how many times people have had sessions with me and send me a piece of paper with a whole bunch of words and tell me that's their marketing plan - and after reading the first 30 words, I realize that it isn't?

I've received outlines of tasks, brain dump ideas with no clarity, and lists of media wishes. After going through this so many times, it was clear to me that most people don't understand what marketing is. They come with a lot of ideas, but do not realize that marketing isn't working for them because they simply don't know what it is.

It's difficult to grasp the concept of marketing if you have wrong information. So, one of the first things I ask clients is what it is that they want to do. Most of the time their answer is "I just need marketing." But they don't know what that actually looks like. Or they think marketing equates to a colorful website with a snazzy matching logo and cute flyers. It's like putting the cart before the horse but wondering why it isn't pulling!

But I want to tell you what it is, and marketing is the back-end work that helps you connect to your consumer. It's finding out what makes your offer (I may interchangeably use this word in place of product or service) important enough for people to buy from you. Marketing isn't "toss it on the ceiling hoping it sticks!" You have to be strategic with the colors, fonts, styles, etc. used, and know how to use the "answers" from the research to find out what connects people to what you offer.

And I can also tell you that many do not want to do the back-end work because it is a lot of work, and it takes time! Marketing research can take at *least* six weeks to complete. And if you're doing a 6-week research project, you can get polls or surveys done and about 15-20 interviews with vendors, industry colleagues, etc. (we'll discuss that more later). Then you have to dissect that data and categorize by need (or challenge) as well as demographic variables: age, race, gender, financial base, hobbies, occupation, etc.

The research is just the first part of it, then you have to align that data to build a relationship with your avatar – or ideal client – in a way that you can attract them to get them to buy. This includes the flyers, emails, campaigns, etc. It's important to know how your website should be attractive to your audience and to potential clients or customers. You want to make it user-friendly and clean; no one will go on a scavenger hunt to find a sale! Once you know the habits of your ideal clients, then you know how to speak their sales language – that is marketing!

The type of marketing is also misunderstood. Although the foundation is about the same, it isn't cookie-cutter for all things and industries. The process of email marketing is different from sales marketing. I find that many people try to apply sales marketing variables to social media marketing, and when it fails, they automatically dismiss it by saying it does not work for them. It isn't that the process did not work, they just didn't know what they were doing. Oftentimes, business owners will catch free training, and take basic information to try to apply to unique campaigns. Tools can sometimes operate differently when applied under unique circumstances. The process may not always align with the goals of the campaign, and when marketing tactics are used incorrectly, it tends to not yield the expected results.

Understanding what marketing is, and how to do it effectively takes time, practice, and strategy. The key word to this is strategy! The reason the investment is heavy is because the back-end work is strategic and takes time to review and implement. There are so many moving pieces to marketing, and if you haven't obtained the knowledge, skill, and experience, you will forever think that marketing is hard. You will always struggle in that area of your business, and you will continue to digest wrong information that does not work with your business model or your goals. Now let's talk about how that wrong information hurts your business.

Listening to the Wrong Information

Can you believe that I have had people who say they are in marketing but don't actually know what marketing is, then try to instruct other people on how to do marketing for their business? It happens all of the time, and I have to unravel the cords of incorrect information often.

It's frustrating when you don't know what you're doing, then mimicking what you think someone else is doing, and it still doesn't work! But we fail to know the back-end of how people get magnificent results. All we know is "I have a business, and I need marketing now!" The *how* and *where* are always the big important ingredients that seem to get lost in the recipe.

So what are some myths or errors that we often hear when it comes to marketing?

1. **Marketing is about having a website**. The purpose of your website is not to just market your business. So many people get a website set up and do nothing with it. It just sits there. And then they get frustrated with paying for a domain of a site they feel isn't benefiting them. And that's

understandable! They were given the wrong information thinking that just having the website was going to catapult their business revenue. No one told them that they have to work on strategies to get people attracted to the website, and they have to make it engaging by having some content that encourages their decision to buy (i.e. lead magnet downloads).

2. **Marketing works itself.** Posting and dropping is not going to be meat to a hungry lion. Trends change constantly, so how are you competing with others in your industry? How are you weeding through the overwhelming messaging to speak direct and clearly to your ideal customer? This just doesn't happen on its own. It requires work, thought, and work again.

3. **Marketing happens overnight.** In 30 days you will be a swinging 6-figure chick – lies! Did you know it took three years before Jay-Z got his first hit single? No? Did you know Amazon was mocked for years as being a joke in e-commerce, but 9 years later they became the central station of e-commerce generating billions of dollars a year? Success in marketing is not microwaveable where you add

graphics and stir. Marketing is the stuff you do behind the scenes.

4. **Content creation is the same as marketing.** As we get deeper into this book, you'll find out that marketing is more about relationships than it is about visible tangibles. Content creation can be used to market an idea, product, or service, but it does not define the concept and practice of marketing.

5. **Promotion and marketing is the same thing.** These two practices often get mixed up for small business owners, and they tend to merge them or think they are one and the same. The main difference between the two is this: marketing is about the identification of the needs of your customer, while promotion is about showcasing the experience to the customer.

6. **If I need marketing, then I definitely need PR (public relations).** This is not necessarily true. PR is about image-building while marketing is more about relationship to the sale. Does PR help with sales? Sure it does, but that's not the main focus of PR. The two work together very well, but it's not necessary that you have to have PR if you're creating a marketing strategy or plan. At some point, you

may want to scale your business and do more with your product or services that may require you to invest in publicity; but it's not a necessity to have it.

7. **Marketing is limited to social media.** This is a huge misconception about marketing that has been nearly drilled into small business owner's minds for the last 15 years. Although social media has become one of the chief "hubs" for marketing and it has become vital to have a social media presence, it is not the only place you can market your product or service. We'll address this more later.

Now that we've discussed some of the myths, let's look at some other wrong information that may be shared regarding marketing.

How many people have you heard say that marketing is for large corporations or you have to have been in business for a while before you take on marketing? I've heard it. And it surprises me every time I hear it.

Anyone who is looking to sell a service or product should incorporate marketing into their plans. It doesn't matter if your business is 3-months old or 30 years old, or if you're an online etsy business or a large corporate board-governed conglomerate. Marketing is an important component that will help you develop revenue and develop the right offers for your customers or clients. It is something that you need to invest in at any and all stages of your business development.

As your business matures, the more extensive and detailed you will need to get with your marketing. But the basics of marketing are all the same no matter how big your business is or how old it is. The level of metrics you have for a 7-figure corporation won't be the same level of metrics for a first year online business, but that doesn't mean you don't need metrics to evaluate what worked and what didn't work in your strategy or your campaign. The more money that's involved, the more work that's required.

Another piece of bad advice when it comes to marketing is when people tell others that you have to "fake it until you make it." Not only is that untrue, but it can be misleading to your customers and will undo all of the work you've put into connecting with your audience. You always want to be authentic and do the work! Do the research! *Don't create products and services for non-existent people; it won't work!* Marketing is about getting to know the people you want to buy from you – so why would you lie to them? Never ever tell a customer something false about your product or service just to get their money. People see through that real fast and in the social media world, that labels you as a scam artist fast and in a hurry.

Marketing should never be about "telling people what they want to hear," but should be about sharing with them how your offer will help them with their problem. Having listening skills is top-tier in marketing. It is important to hear what your audience is saying – good and bad, because it helps you to improve your messaging, your approach, and your offer. Your position with your marketing is not to force people to buy from you, but to make it known to them that you have what they need to fix their problem.

Another piece of wrong information is that everybody is your audience. What about this: "You can sell anything to anybody." That is so far from the truth! Remember, marketing and promoting are two different things. Yes, you can promote to anybody, but marketing? No. Marketing is about finding out who needs what you have to offer. Your friends, your family, and your community may or may not be the people who will buy from you genuinely. I said genuinely, because sometimes our family and friends will support us just to help, but they don't necessarily buy it because it's something they need. And they rarely become return customers or nurtured customers. Our target market is often skewed because we don't know how to use marketing correctly and effectively, so when we have been in business for a month and no one buys from us, we're sad and ready to quit, yet we haven't done our own homework in our business! We've listened to the lies and perpetuated unhealthy or incorrect marketing tactics, failing before we could even get started.

That "build it, and they will come" is a tactic in marketing that will leave you broke! Remember, you are in business to solve a PROBLEM. That means that you have something that people need and want. Creating products or services that you deem as "medicine" for people that you THINK are "sick," is a set up for failure. This is why research is so important. People are initially in the market for solutions to problems they have already acknowledged. If they have not acknowledged that they have a problem, guess what, they won't come looking for a solution. You're in a pool of other businesses and brands that offer solutions to problems. Marketing isn't a magnet that simply hypnotizes and draws people to you. It is a tool that helps you identify the right ones that need your help.

Online entrepreneurship has changed the course of how marketing is done. With so much overwhelming messaging due to the growing platforms to promote on, along with the ease of access to those platforms, it can be challenging and people can become desperate in how they get their messaging out or become quick on the trigger in how they reach their audience. But with true marketing, it takes patience and commitment to the process. During the first part of the 19th century, advertising was huge and promotion began to spring legs at the close of the century. Now, in the 21st century, marketing has become more critical than ever. But if you don't have the right information or the right tools in how to implement marketing for your business, the challenge will be greater and you'll likely struggle in generating sales.

The Importance of Marketing

All business owners *know* they need marketing, but they don't really take it seriously in developing their business. They confuse promotion with marketing, and are so quick to give up (we'll talk more on that later).

Let's take a look at how critical marketing is to not only your business growth, but your sales and revenue. In this section, we're going to ask a series of questions regarding the importance of marketing.

How do you get people to know what you sell? Do you drop and leave waiting for them to come to you? How do they know who you are? Are they even in need of what you just dropped? How do you know? Marketing is the tool that helps you to answer these questions with the *right* answers.

Who are you selling to? Have you ever sat in a class at school and was bored out of your mind because the lecture wasn't interesting or you did not feel the information was relevant to you, so you zoned out or just left? That's what happens when we blindly promote to audiences. Marketing is important in helping you understand who is asking for your offer, who needs what you offer, and how they want to use what you offer.

What are people buying? Trends are oftentimes seen as flighty or trivial, but to a business owner, they are like liquid gold. Understanding what's hot and what's not is a part of marketing research. If you don't have this information, how do you know *when* to market your offer? People aren't going to buy something they aren't interested in.

Where in the world can people buy from you? Marketing research is key to help with knowing where your leads and potential customers are, so you know where to put it before their eyes. If your target market frequents the Facebook marketplace, why would you advertise it heavily on Twitter? It's less likely they will go to Twitter (or if they aren't on Twitter at all) to see your offer and buy it when they are asking about it. If your market isn't really on digital platforms, why would you promote daily on social media? They aren't going to see it!! But you won't know this, unless you do the marketing research and get to know your audience's habits and needs.

Next: What is it about your offer that people like? Marketing is a gamechanger! Remember we talked about relationships? This is where this component steps in. Having a fancy and crafty name is one thing, and definitely plays a role in branding, but you have to know what people will buy. You have to research and communicate with your audience on what people like. What you offer should be something that is easy for people to access, it should address their problem or want quickly. It should be something different, innovative, and creative. You have to give people something good to talk about.

Does it matter how I sell it? Marketing plays a role in helping you to know how to package your product or service. It's important to take that data and apply it to your marketing strategy and plan. Does your audience prefer digital products or physical products – or do they like both? What does your audience think about videos? Let's give an example. I worked for a lawn care product company, and the majority of the company's buyers were elderly, and they often complained about how the bags were hard to open. And although they felt it was a good product, they were discouraged from buying because it was so hard to rip open the bags. And some did not like the bottle design of the liquid fertilizer. They said it was hard to grip when applying to their flower gardens. The company invested this information from their market and eventually created a new easy grip design bottle that many loved! The customers felt heard and catered to, and continued to buy. This was definitely a win!

How are you nurturing your customers? Implementing good marketing is how you will know how to take it to the next level with your customers. Marketing helps to build repeat customers and referrals. When you go the extra mile, people appreciate you understanding and tending to their needs. People like to know that their money with your business matters and that you actually care about fixing their problem over just making a sale. Marketing can also help you customize products and services, provide options and accessibility to your business and brand. Knowing that their feelings matter is how you build and sustain income in your business. And how do you find this out? You guessed it: marketing. Take Rihanna's company Savage X Fenty for example. She makes lingerie for all body types. A huge portion of her demographic are full-figured women. Do you remember what her company's early ads looked like? Slender shaped women with perfect, flat stomachs and model-looking bodies. Women commented on her ads saying they liked the lingerie and liked Rihanna, but wished they could find something in their size. So what happened next? We started to see more ads with women with "everyday" full-figured bodies wearing sexy and classy lingerie in different sizes and styles. Gone were the plain "granny" style underwear for full-figured women, because Savage X Fenty had come to the rescue. Sales in this demographic soared simply because they took what their audience said as research to nurture their customers. Her company's motto even speaks to the nurturing of her audience: "Celebrates fearlessness and **inclusivity**: We got something for everybody." This will also help us in answering the next question.

How are you scaling your product or service? First let's define scaling in business. It means to grow your business without having to spend more money to do it, in which the endgame makes you more money. Another part of that is when you don't have to exhaust additional resources to grow in your business. Knowing how to achieve company goals, you need resources and data. You want to be able to use low cost platforms and resources to do these two things: meet company goals and to increase your bottom line.

Marketing, promotion, and advertising is key in helping to get this done. When you've exhausted your campaign and exceeded your past goals, using marketing to scale your business is where you should turn: new data and updates on the needs of your audience. Creating evergreen offers with your already high ticket offers can be done successfully when you know how you can further nurture your customers; and we already know where this data comes from: marketing.

Don't Know Your Audience

If I had a dollar for every small business owner that says no one is buying their products and they're ready to close shop after being in business for less than one year, or they're mad because no one supports them after the first week of their launch; I'd be a trillionaire by now.

When you fail to do the work, you fall victim to believing that just because you have the "latest" product or a "new" product, everybody should just buy from you - simply because you're YOU. And to be realistic, you may find that Mama will buy to support her baby, but on the grand scale, no one is buying from you "just because." That's why mindset is important. Ask yourself, are you in business because you simply want to get a bag to floss or are you in business because you see a need and you want to be the one to bring the solution?

Doing the research is how you discover who your audience (or ideal customer) is, not scrolling through your phone to drop spam ads! The drop-and-scam type of "marketing" hinders your sales and boxes you in on how to develop products and services that are attractive, trustworthy, and relevant. You cut yourself short on getting to know the actual people who need what you offer, because you're stuck on trying to force-feed your products or services to people who have no relationship to what you offer and only have a relationship to you.

And understanding who your audience is goes past simple demographics. You have to know how to use the data you have. Have you ever heard of the Know, Like, and Trust Factor? (KLT) It is a tool used in marketing to segment data on your audience to build a relationship between them and your offer. Building this is not an easy feat. It takes time, testing, and more work. A business starting out automatically thinks they know what's good for everyone, so they try to sell to everyone. And when no one buys what they offer, they're ready to quit or get upset because no one buys. I remember a coach once told me, "If you try to sell to everyone, you're selling to no one." And those words are ever more true in running a business. Remember we talked about mindset? A business owner's mindset has to change to thinking more on quality than quantity. Having more followers, more members in your social media groups, or more likes does not equate to more sales. It just means you have crowded rooms.

So why aren't your friends buying from you? Well, do they actually need what you're offering? Were they part of your focus group or research for the offer? If not, why would they buy it? Just because they know you? Is that why you're in business - to sell to people that know you or are you in business to sell to people who actually have a need and you have their solution?

This is why research is important. The research serves as your guide for your offer. That data helps you know who you need to serve, why you need to serve them, and what they need. Once you have that data, you can create a plan or strategy to establish relationships with them to get them to pay attention to what you have and how you can relate to their needs. People are more comfortable with people that seem "real" and authentic. They aren't too interested in people who pour so much energy and time into pseudo-success. They want to know that people are genuine, that they care, that they understand, and that they have a solution.

Here are some tips on how to build your KLT factor:

- **Share your personal story.** What were your struggles? How were you able to overcome it? What was your victory? Share your "why". What was the reason for starting this business? How does that connect with your offer?

- **Give samples or snippets.** Depending on what your offer is, let people sample it! Give freebies in exchange for an email address to add them to your leads list. That way you can communicate with them and nurture them more.

- **Go Live and have a conversation.** Talk about problems your audience is having. Get their feedback and ask about what solutions they need. This can be referenced in your video, then offer the solution – your offer!

This helps build relationships and get your audience comfortable with you and generates brand awareness of your offer.

Another step in building that trust is making sure you have systems in place to give your customers a great experience through customer service. Many small business owners do not understand how this plays a role in marketing. Remember, you're building your relationship with your audience – not your mother, best friend, or church member.

How customers experience you is important to your marketing strategy. What people like, what people know, and how well they trust is very important to *your* business. The experience is what impresses upon your audience. And how do you do that? With marketing. The more you know about who your audience is and what makes them "buy," the better you will be in selling your offer.

Marketing v. The Microwave

One of the biggest myths of marketing is that it's a quick fix to boosting sales. The stages of marketing can be intense and time-consuming. I've had clients who were onboarded and expected to generate big digit sales within 30 days. But there are some problems with this dream goal: (1) they don't have a defined audience of people who are ready to buy, (2) no one knows who they are, and (3) they don't have a structured plan to promote the offer.

They come with a plan to just toss it on the wall, hoping it sticks and a marketing strategist to slap the glue on it (remember we talked about this before?). But that's not how successful marketing works, and forging ahead with this plan is a recipe for disaster. The snap-crackle-pop idea of marketing doesn't exist, and it needs to be expelled.

So, why do people think marketing is something that's quick and easy? I believe it's because business owners, especially those who are new, tend to see the end-result of marketing with other people's businesses, and think that it's easy and simple. I also think that people simply don't know how to create a real strategy – or understand what strategy means. I've had experiences where I've been sent outlines of tasks, but no strategy; no why; no step-by-step plan; no end result. Just a list of to-do's and desires. Another reason I believe business owners think marketing is easy is because they don't understand how campaigns work. Marketing is about order. Your strategy is the blueprint, but your campaign is the action plan. Without the harmony between the two, marketing won't be as easy as it looks.

And patience is a virtue. It is definitely a gem to have when it comes to marketing. There is no osmosis or magic to marketing. When creating a strategy, you want to make sure you include the time to get it done. Remember, it takes time to get people to notice you, like you, and trust you – *before* they buy.

The assumption is that if you make it, they will buy it. But who is buying it? And if you know, do you know when they're ready to buy? How would you know that? I can tell you; marketing. If you don't already have an audience or you don't know who needs what you have, then how long do you even know how quick it will take for people to purchase?

One question I always ask clients is: Do you already have an email list? Or do you already have an active group? If not, then you're starting from ground zero (which is okay) and you are not going to be able to market successfully within one month. It's going to take time – especially if you don't have any evidence that potential customers can look to in order to trust you (i.e. testimonials, case studies, media coverage, etc.). That's why it's important to create a plan! Set aside time and make sure your goals are clear. Just wanting to make quick money is not good enough. If you're serious about marketing your business, there is no microwave plan that will work or work effectively. You have to understand that rushing anything doesn't produce faster results; it actually can cause you to miss out on some important parts of your campaign.

Don't Know the Basics

Many people struggle with marketing because they don't understand the basics. If you don't know the fundamentals, it's going to be hard to know how to do the work. We discussed the myths of marketing earlier in this book, but now we are going to dig into the real deal of marketing.

For one, marketing is a partnership. The strategist doesn't do all of the work alone. You as the client must put forth just as much energy, effort, and action into marketing. Your strategist may ask you questions about your business, and it behooves you to answer them, and answer them as honestly as possible. This is your business, and there is no shame in not knowing something or understanding why something is an important part of growing your business' image or connection with your audience. Marketing isn't a delegated service; it's a partnership.

Deliverables are important. Building a brand is an ever-growing journey, but you need to know where to begin. Making sure your messaging and assets "match" is a part of the marketing strategy conversation. As a business, having your hex codes (color palette numbers), brand sheets, product credentials and projections, etc. are critical pieces to have ready to get started on building a strategy.

Relationships are about familiarity and consistency. So let's look at an example: McDonald's. I like using this company for example because of how they encompass the picture of good marketing and branding. Their colors are yellow, red, and white. When you look at the playground furniture it's yellow. The logo is placed strategically in various places throughout the dining room. The main theme with all of their food items, specials, and programs center around family and fun. This is how McDonald's has maintained their popularity. They connect with their customers through marketing on a consistent basis that continues to scale with each generation of customers. If you don't get anything else from this section, understand that if your marketing assets are cohesive and match, customers become more and more familiar with you and comfortable with your business to be repeat customers.

Setting goals with your marketing is just as key as setting overall business goals. You want to have a clear direction of where you want to go with your offer as well as why you're marketing your offer in the first place. For example: Do you want to build your residual income with repeat customers? Is this a nurturing offer to further service existing customers? Are you promoting a new offer? Are you wanting to meet a certain sales goal? If you are, you have to be realistic and specific. Saying you want to make "six figures" is not specific. Don't be afraid to put a number on it.

And the question is, are six figures even realistic and doable at the current stage you're at in your business? If you just started your business three months ago, that's not an attainable goal. Marketing strategies and campaigns should address short-term goals, because you will always be evolving and scaling your offer as you grow in your business. Always be as specific as you can with your goals.

"Grill down" your goals with questions until you've gotten to the bare bones.

Once you set your goal and know who you're wanting to reach, next you want to know how long is it going to take to reach that goal. This is why the research is important. Examining competitors and the trends of your audience comes into play with this part of strategizing. A good rule of thumb is a strategy can be created within 2 months and a campaign 3 months, but a great strategy can be done 3 months ahead of launch while the campaign should be done at least 6 months to a year. A year is best to give you time to repeat your messaging enough to your audience! Remember, it takes at least 7 times for a customer to hear and see your message before they settle on a decision to buy from you. Repeat messaging also puts people in the mindset that you're consistent about your approach and not a one-time drop and move type of business that isn't that concerned about wooing them for their support. That messaging can be from social media ads, commercials, videos, webinars, etc.

After finding out how long it's going to take for you to reach your goal, you want to schedule a specific release or launch date. This is important because you want to make sure you're paying attention to trends, holidays, etc. You also want to use data that you collected on your audience's buying habits and include this in determining your release or launch date. For example: A famous entertainer released an album and although the content was awesome, the date they selected to release it was overshadowed by a well-known festival. A good marketing strategist pays attention to trends and advises on the right time to release or launch.

You also want to make sure you have metrics in place. This is important to guide you on what's working in your strategy and campaign and what's not. You want to measure each part and align that with how well your audience is receiving your strategies and how well the tasks on your campaign are converting. Remember your goals! You want to make sure you are always looking back to your goals to make sure you're meeting each milestone to the finish and not getting off track.

It's important to revisit your metric results after your campaign is done. Evaluate what worked, when it worked, and who it worked for. You want to measure this so you can take this data along to know how to nurture or scale up your offer. You have to take into account every piece of your strategy and campaign. This includes the quality of your graphics, fonts, colors, video captions, hashtags, price points, the time of day you advertised, posted, or went live, and the places you shared your content.

There are a number of things that it takes to design and implement a marketing campaign, but these are the basic things to do that can ensure that you're off to a great start.

Businesses That Are Not Coachable

Even with a great plan at hand, another problem business owners have with getting marketing is that they struggle with being coached. It all starts with the mindset. If you come to the table with the mentality that you already know what marketing is and how to do it, but struggle with being successful in it, it's going to be difficult to listen to someone who comes in to help.

Coaching other entrepreneurs can be a challenge, because they already have the mindset that they are in control of their business and know what they want, even when they really don't. If business owners aren't ready to listen and learn because they think they are the ones in control, they will struggle when a marketing professional tries to redirect them for the betterment of their business. This kind of thinking tends to be a huge blocker when it comes to business growth, not only regarding marketing, but in growing, period.

Oftentimes business owners look up to those who provide supposed "guarantees" or "quick fixes" with financial records counting as results. And when their mind is filled with these things, it's hard to be coached to do things a different way.

Another reason that makes business owners uncoachable, is when they hire subcontractors or consultants they often treat them as employees instead of business collaborators. This can block them from readily receiving coaching or advice because they struggle with respecting the expertise of their consultant as their equal. Internet gurus have somewhat spoiled business owners with quick fixes and picture perfect results, yet they neglect to showcase the actual "work" that goes into marketing.

A marketing professional's social proof or popularity can also hinder business owners from being coachable. If it's not someone who is internet famous or an influencer in the industry, they may not see the value of someone who actually has knowledge and training. Remember, marketing is not some glamorous showpiece for sales. It's the behind-the-scenes work that helps make sales happen. Marketing drives the ship, and is often not on display when it comes to the success of a business. Yet, those who understand marketing and how business relationships work, know that if a campaign is successful, it's because the marketing was done correctly - and done well.

Trust in business is a critical, yet delicate, commodity. It is something hard to obtain, especially with strangers. If you're unsure if listening to a marketing consultant, strategist, or coach is the best thing for you to do, always ask for references, their portfolio, case studies,or testimonials from former clients. Build that trust early on, because your marketing professional will serve as your right hand for the sales process of your offer. You want someone you can trust, and someone you're willing to humble yourself with, to listen to, and follow directions.

Being coachable means being flexible. Marketing is one of those industries that is tied to trends. The needs of your customers can sometimes be finicky, so you have to stay abreast on the ebbs and flows of what they want and need - and when. But if you have it already made up in your mind that you're only going to do one thing, one thing only and one way only, you're setting yourself up for a struggle in marketing your offer.

Being coachable also means that you come with no preconceived notions about what marketing is and how marketing fits into your business. If you know so much about marketing, why hire a consultant? You have to toss aside what you think you know, and trust the expertise of your consultant. Sometimes your goals may not align with how marketing works in your business, and they need to be re-adjusted or even scrapped all together; and that's okay!

In review, the greatest two stumbling blocks in a business owner not being coachable when it comes to marketing rest in their mindset where they think they already know what marketing is and how it works, and being misled by the glamour of end-game results instead of paying attention to what isn't being said or explained. It's important to know the why and the how when it comes to trusting the marketing expertise of a consultant. Be clear in knowing that when they join your team, they are not your subordinates or employees where you get to delegate and boss them around. They are important teachers to help guide you through the process of establishing relationships with your audience to get them to purchase your offer.

Lazy Businesses Can't Grasp Marketing

I've heard this many times: "I just can't get this marketing thing. It doesn't work for me."

But in my experience, I've learned that it translates to "I just don't want to do the work to completely and successfully market my business." Marketing is not a one-drop shop where you just hand over the reins of your business to an expert. Divatudes don't work well in marketing, because of the intense work that is involved. You want to make sure you're coming ready to listen, provide deliverables, follow recommendations, and offer – as well as – solicit feedback.

The lack of understanding marketing is one of the main culprits for lazy business owners. It's not a flash in the pan tactic to business growth. In my experience, I've had clients tell me how to market their business, and like a fool, I listened to them against my expertise and better judgment all because I wanted to get paid. And I was doing a disservice to my brand and to my client! My own mindset had to change, because I was being lazy! If I'm the expert, then I need to put my foot down and let them know that their ideology is a train wreck, which is why they hired me in the first place.

I've been treated like an "employee" more times than I can count, and it took a serious wake-up call to my own business that I had to change that. I wasn't an employee that just followed orders, I was an expert and my value had to be respected - even with lazy business owners who wanted to be divas. Succumbing to this was proving me to be just as lazy as my clients. I couldn't focus and be successful because of my own indifference to put in the work!

So, what do I mean by being a diva in business? I mean a business owner who snaps their fingers with high-end demands and expects consultants or strategists to just "make it happen." This is how you end up with a struggling business! Whenever I hear "I hired you to do…" but will take no accountability for their own business; that is a recipe for disaster! No one solely has control over *your* business. Technology is very advanced, but it's still quirky. Things happen. Trends change. Tools become obsolete. People are finicky. Investing in the aspects of your business takes more than money. It takes work ethic and sweat equity; and that includes marketing.

Develop great listening skills. This will be one of your greatest assets when it comes to working with a marketing professional. Admit that marketing is not in your wheelhouse, that you need help, and you're open to doing whatever it takes to boost your marketing. (I want to put a quick pin right here: a marketing professional should never be one who is altering or completely changing your business. They should take your goals and transform that data to communicate properly to your audience to optimize them to buy.) Listening for cues and clues can be gems in your business, when you develop and utilize these skills.

That's one of the great things I love about what I do. I'm about collaborating and helping translate a client's ideas and goals in a way that speaks to the right people who will benefit from their offer. And doing that takes work; it takes some deconstructing, listening, being heard, and working together. Marketing doesn't have room for laziness. Marketing isn't one-sided. Laziness delays progress and eventually will kill your idea or offer.

Not Understanding Marketing is Not For the Free

Every aspect of your business requires some type of investment. And marketing is no different. It's one of the most intricate pieces to the sales funnel that most business owners neglect to give it the attention it deserves because narratives and improper teaching have impacted them to believe it doesn't require any money to accomplish it. Lies. All lies.

When you don't see the value in it, you don't appreciate it. We've already established that marketing is a lot of work, and it takes time, ideas, strategy, implementation, and review. And any skill takes experience, time, and technique and should be compensated. Remember we discussed how important marketing is for your business? Since that has been understood, now you have to include it in your budget.

When I first started in this industry I low-balled because I just wanted to get some proof under my belt. But once I realized my own worth and value in what I do, I had to do my own market research to find out how much marketing strategists and consultants actually get paid: the average is to the tune of

$75-$300 an hour. And for single campaign projects, you're looking at anywhere between $1000-$3500. Now watch this: McDonald's spends on average $1 billion a year in marketing and advertising - and that's just in the U.S! The time it takes to actually do the research, filter through the data to create the avatar (or some call ideal customer), brainstorm the strategy, put the campaign together and then implement it....Yeah, it's pricey.

Expecting marketing on the low-low translates (yeah, we do a lot of translating in this book!) to "I don't see the value in my business. I just want to scrape by and not show my customer how important it is to have what I offer." I get it that most business owners start out with $0 to a minimal budget. The focus is usually guided on getting a website and setting up social media platforms. But if there is no investment on creating the process on how to get those products or services before the right people, what good is having a website and posting on social media?

Every business should create an item for marketing in their monthly budget. It should be treated just like domain costs, software, professional portfolios, etc. Remember, it's just that important! Now, if you're just starting out and don't really have the budget for top-tier marketing, don't expect top-tier sales in your business, and it's okay. Start where you are and set realistic and valuable goals in that space. But don't neglect to invest in marketing. It will be stressful and discouraging because you won't get the results you expect.

You never want to have top-tier expectations with a low investment. It is imbalanced thinking and will show up heavily in your customer service, your presentation and promotions, and your networking principles. And who wants to buy from someone who skates and scams on the value of the business? No one I know! It shows entrepreneurial immaturity (and it doesn't matter how long you've been legally in business) when you don't expect to pay for the value of help, but expect customers to pay top dollar for your offer's value. It's not good business sense, and it shortchanges you in the end. You remember the saying, "You get what you pay for?" Even if someone does a great job for the "low", you're still shortchanging your business. Why? Can I tell it like it is? Because even the best professional doesn't perform 100% when they don't feel respected or valued. The devalue opens the door to conflict, stubbornness, miscommunication, and stress.

Always budget for marketing. Be ready with each promotion and each launch to put forth some money on tools. Be ready to invest in someone's time and expertise to help you navigate those tools to create the best strategy, campaign, or funnel for your business. When you treat marketing as something that's important to your business, you will value it more and get the best value for your business.

Not Understanding Trends

Marketing practices are as old as the Italian city of Pompeii during the late B.C. era. As tribal identifications and practices became the norm in the intermingling of other nations, marketing and branding practices became even more necessary and pronounced. Consumer culture continued to grow after the 12th century, so the need to distinguish and compete became even more evident for businesses.

Today, it is as common as breathing, and industries have become so saturated and crowded, that marketing is almost the lifeline to a business' success or failure. To understand how marketing works, you need to understand how trends play a big role in how your marketing strategy should be developed.

The word *trend* comes from the German word meaning "evolve." To build a KLT factor with your audience, you need to make sure you're staying updated on what's popping and what's not. Trends are very important because they allow businesses to broaden perimeters in their industry with their market, and give businesses real-time access into what their audience likes and are interested in. Trends are a very neat tool to use when you're doing your market research, and are very helpful when you're looking for ways to nurture leads and existing customers; so don't sleep on it!

One of the errors businesses make when it comes to trends is they look at it as "I'm not trying to do what everyone else is doing," so they ignore trend research all together, but struggle in connecting with their audience. They tend to try and serve EVERYBODY with a dollar, believing if they cast their net wide, they will generate more sales. But that's quite the opposite. Casting blindly and widely brings in people who have no connection and no desire to buy from you. This tends to push out the people who want to hear and see your offer and those that are ready to buy.

Another problem is businesses use trends to compete with those who they should be collaborating with (we'll discuss more on this in an upcoming section). They tend to neglect their own audience for trying to grab the spot of someone else's audience. I call this 'marketing suicide' because you can kill your audience before you even get started. Many first-year business owners experience marketing suicide, simply because they aren't being consistent in focusing on what their audience wants. Remember when I said people are finicky? It's true! Today Birkin bags are popping and next quarter it will be something else. If you're in the fashion accessories business, don't you think it would behoove you to know this? If you're still selling bags that were hot last quarter as a high ticket item, and people are talking about Burberry, you'll start to get discouraged when your sales drop dramatically. It's because you're not paying attention to the trends of your industry and what your audience is talking about. Am I saying that you won't have days, weeks, months, where your sales aren't top tier? No, but at least you can stay relevant with your customers and they can see that you actually are attentive to their wants. That's cultivating their purchase power, and you want that!

Another issue I see with how businesses treat trends is that they are last in getting low-hanging fruit because they choose not to utilize trends in their marketing. What I mean by this is, if businesses are paying attention to trending topics, products, services, issues, etc. they can get the jump on being 'first' or the 'plug' when it comes to certain products. Even if you don't generate sales every single time with every single person, you have the next best thing: leads (Know this: leads aren't just service-connected)! And you can drop them into your sales funnel to nurture them along until they're ready to turn into paying customers. Even if leads don't turn into paying customers, they can turn into referrals simply because they trust how you stay connected with their wants and needs. And we know how word of mouth still works, right? Right.

Don't Know Where to Market

It's 2023, and do you know that with over 33 million small business owners in the U.S., a lot of them STILL don't know where to do their marketing. They have been given incorrect information, thinking only social media is the end-all be-all place to be! And guess what, they miss out!

It's important to be versatile in where you choose to market. First thing is you have to know where your people are. How many of you have planned a party at an empty venue expecting people to already be there? Listen, as a small business owner, you have to go where your people are! You have to listen to their conversation, their habits, their hobbies (sounds like that research kicking in again!), etc. Social media is an excellent place to market your business and market to your audience, but it isn't the ONLY place. Boxing your business in one platform will cause you to miss out on leads and customers that you never imagined existed. I want to share with you a few places that small businesses should add to their list when it comes to marketing their offer:

1. **Search Engines.** Did you know you can register your business on Google? Not only does this drive traffic to your website, but it also gives your business a professional look and adds to your company's social proof. I know you've heard people on TV say, "Google me." Yeah, that's it. Now, my PR side is about to come out on this. When you have testimonials, have customers share them on your Google page, add pictures, photos, graphics, use backlinks, etc. to help push you up in the search engine. So when people are looking for experts or specific products, guess who pops up on the first page? Yeah, you.

2. **Online Directories.** Yelp, Angie's List, BBB, Yahoo, Bing for Business, Whitepages, etc. are some great platforms to market your business on. You want to make sure that you're making sure to choose ones that will benefit your audience the most.

3. **Social Media.** This one is a no-brainer. But I want to drop this science for you. Not all channels cater to your business. Do the research! Know where your audience hangs out at. Know statistics and insights to each platform, like we all know Facebook caters to middle-aged, family-oriented people. Instagram is the millennial station. Twitter is for the

corporate professional. It's not to say that your audience may not be found on any cross-channels, but you want to make sure your strategy is heavy on the channels where the majority of your audience hangs out.

4. **Websites.** I know plenty of business owners who don't see their website as a place to do marketing. They have no clue how to use SEO, keywords, strategic positioning, etc. to grab their customers. And those things are different for each business and for each audience. Again, this is why market research is so important.

5. **Digital and paper media.** Newspapers, magazines, radio and TV stations may have lost some sauce, but they still slap when it comes to marketing. Media ads *still* work. Don't sleep on paying for those ads. Even social media ads bring in new leads, subscribers, and customers. Research your market and know what platforms will get the most eyes from your customers.

6. **Blogs.** About 5 years ago, blogs were hot. Do you remember when you would go to a blog and the entire left side of the blog was lit up with ads? They may not be as hot as back then, but they still are a viable place to market your business.

7. **Community Boards.** Libraries used to be a big spot to visit when you were looking for a job or needing help. Some libraries still have that service board back by the restrooms. Places of worship and laundromats have them too. And don't forget digital community boards like Craigslist, professional group boards, and city calendars.

Knowing the *how* is definitely important, but if you don't know the *where*, you're still losing out. Get a full picture and be ready to do some powerhouse marketing!

Don't Know the Difference Between Competition and Tribe

With the emergence of e-commerce and online businesses, opportunities to make money in business industries have become easier to do as well as insurmountable. No longer do you have to have huge start-up costs or certain things in place to start a business such as a building, office furniture, employees, etc. In 2022, small businesses surged up to 5 billion. With this level of competition, small business owners operate in fear. They think that if they expand their network, their ideas or business will be stolen or capitalized on. This fear tends to create a feeling of hostility and defensiveness that hurts the business owner's opportunities to connect with others in the industry to build their business and grow your leads.

So, what does this have to do with marketing? Building a tribe is another way to narrow down and get to know your audience. This is a great tool when marketing on social media. Social media is the new "hub" and hangout for people – business owners and consumers. Joining groups, community pages, or rooms (Clubhouse) where your customers hang out is key to learning more about them, what they need, what they're not liking, etc. When questions come up in groups, a great marketing tip is to provide feedback that helps to bring awareness to who you are and what you do, so people can build trust with you. Have you heard of the phrase, the more you know the more you grow? Building tribes also help you to sharpen your expertise. You may think this applies more to service-based offers, but product-based businesses can take advantage of tribe building as well. Needing vendor lists, connections, tips on how to manage your e-commerce store, etc.? It's important to know people in your industry that you can glean from, and see where you can fill in the gap, scale, or repurpose with your products/services.

Negatively assessing competition is a time-waster, and it separates you from opportunities that can help you nurture and grow your own customer base. Business owners that behave negatively regarding other businesses in their industry don't pay attention to what their own audience wants, because they're too busy catering to and focusing on what someone else's brand is doing.

Even if you sell the same thing as someone else, what you do and how you do it, makes all of the difference. Don't be a lazy entrepreneur and think business is cut-and-paste or cookie-cutter. Build relationships and network with competitors so you're able to expand your reach, learn of different ways to meet your customers' needs by doing something different than what your competition is doing, and sharpen your understanding of the language in your industry.

Competition can definitely inspire innovation, but one of the main differences between tribes and competition is priority. Competitors look for ways on how to out-do or one-up the other company. They're focused more on quantity; the more money they make, the more followers they have, the more engagement they receive, the better and more successful they feel they are as a business. Tribes look for better ways to expand their quality. They want to improve quality of products/services, network, their overall business culture and customer service. They look to others in their industry as goalposts or "markers" to improve. They become more confident in what they offer than looking at how much they offer – this is a nugget of wisdom when it comes to marketing! Your customers don't want you fighting over them with other businesses; they just want you to take care of *them*.

Closing Remarks

I've said a great bit to explain the reasons marketing may have not been working for you. I hope that you take what was said and apply it. Make changes in your business because you want to see yourself be successful and you want to fulfill a need in serving others.

Remember: *relationship, relationship, relationship* is the heart of marketing. People buy from PEOPLE they know, like, and trust. They don't spend their coins with products, they spend it with people. Everything else surrounds mindset. To be successful with marketing is about empowering your mind with the mechanics and it puts you ahead of the game by the time you're ready to onboard a marketing professional with your team, and that's why I'm writing this book; I want you to succeed!

My theory about marketing is taking exposure along with relationships and transforming that into sales. This formula is key to the success of your business regardless of the type of model you have. The choice is yours and the bag is for the taking. Choose wisely.

Business Terms & Terminologies:

Growing in business means learning about business. Understanding the language sets you apart and helps you to be able to have a worthy seat at the table when it comes to negotiating and vetting members of your team. Here are a few terms with explanations and examples to help provide you with a clear understanding of who and how you need to build your team.

Marketing: The steps to promote a product or service through research and relationship building.

Branding: The process of making an idea, product, or service identifiable and relatable to an intended audience.

Brand Ambassador: Usually a well-known person who is compensated to endorse or promote a particular company's product or service.

Influencer: A person of notoriety that partners with a company to advertise their products or services by reviews, content creation, or promotion (i.e. contests, giveaways).

Publicist: A person who is hired by a brand or company to help establish and/or maintain good relationships with media organizations and professionals, and manage the image/brand of a company. They sometimes represent the company and analyze the impact of their products or services with their audience.

Marketng strategist: They are responsible for researching and developing comprehensive strategies to communicate and execute a company's goals for their idea, product, or service.

Marketing consultant: A person hired to help a company understand their customers by identifying strengths of a company's product or service to solve a customer's problem.

Marketing coach: A person hired to assist a company meet goals by promoting their strengths (based on their values and mission) in how they meet their customer's needs. They also provide them with tools/skills on how to scale their business.

Social media manager: A person responsible for creating strategies to help meet goals (increase followers, engagement, etc.) through created and executed campaigns, creating engaging content, and reviewing the analytics of the campaign.

Content creator: A person who creates and shares content relevant to a company or brand to educate or entertain audiences.

Email marketing: It is when you send commercial messages (newsletters, alerts, blogs, etc.) to a specific group of people via email to educate or entertain. This is often used to nurture relationships with leads or existing customers.

Social media marketing: The use of social media platforms to promote the sale of a product or service through ads, promotional videos, etc.

Digital marketing: The use of online technology to promote products and services. The two biggest platforms for digital marketing are social media and search engines (i.e. Google, Yelp, Yahoo,etc.).

E-commerce marketing: The practice of using promotional tactics (i.e. SEO, upsells, text messaging, new sales alerts, etc.) to drive traffic to your online store and convert that traffic to paying customers.

Promotion: The act of publicizing a product, service, or idea to a particular audience. This can include sales or discounts, contests, media "plugs", flyers, honorable mentions, etc.

Social Proof: It is the evidence from your company that someone has purchased a product or service, or evidence of a relationship between your brand/company and a media organization or professional.

Advertising: Assets (usually paid) that are produced to promote a product or service to an audience with the intent to convince them to buy. Advertising is not guaranteed sales. This can include billboards, radio spots, newspaper ads, etc.

Scaling: It is the setting up your business to grow without having to increase a substantial amount of resources. For example, spending a considerably low amount of profits to implement a strategy that provides a significant increase in revenue. Spending $5,000 of a $200K profit to make $500K in revenue.

Evergreen: It is usually referred to as a product. It is something you sell (or give as a freebie) and regardless of how old it is, the content is still relevant and does not expire. These types of offers are normally guides, white papers, tutorials, or worksheets that can be sold as low-cost lead magnets or add-ons.

Cost-Efficient Marketing Tools for Start-Up Businesses:

- Excel/Google Sheets
- Trello
- Asana
- Monday
- Survey Monkey
- Make My Persona
- Think (Google Research Tools)
- Canva
- Mailchimp
- Mailerlite
- Vimeo
- (Hubspot) Social Inbox

About the Author

Tonya Franklin is an award-winning best selling author selling in U.S. and European markets. She has been writing since the age of 13, and has had a love for words ever since. She is the BrandCEO of MJS Virtual  Collaborative and the CEO of Imani Blue Books & Press.

Although she expresses herself well as a wordsmith, Tonya has also served as a conference speaker with Black CEO, VA World Conference, The HBCU Tour, CWBN, and Black Business Minded Women's Accelerate. Tonya has experience as a digital magazine contributing writer as well as being the Editor-in-Chief and Founder of the first digital publication for virtual assistants of color.

Tonya loves having ethnic food experiences, serving the community, being an empowerment educator, and advocating for the success of small business.

www.ingramcontent.com/pod-product-compliance
Lightning Source LLC
Chambersburg PA
CBHW072247170526
45158CB00003BA/1022